This is Jesus. God sent Him from heaven to earth. Jesus is God's Son.

Jesus taught people about God. He told them to love each other and be kind.

Jesus healed children and grown-ups who were sick. They thanked Jesus for making them better.

Jesus asked men to follow Him.
They were called His disciples.

Children followed Jesus too.
"Let the children come to me!" He said.

Maze

Help the child find Jesus.

One stormy night,
Jesus told the wind and waves to be still,
and just like that, the sea was calm.
His miracles showed people
that He was God's Son.

Wherever Jesus went, people crowded around Him. They were excited to see the man they had heard so much about.

Jesus said He was the Good Shepherd who would lay down His life for His sheep.

Jesus rode a donkey into the city of Jerusalem. Many people were going there to celebrate a feast.

As Jesus rode into town,
the people waved palm branches.

"Hosanna!"
they shouted.
"Blessed is he
who comes in the
name of the Lord."

What Is Different?

Look at the top image, then circle five things that are different on the bottom image.

Jesus washed His disciples' feet.
Then they shared a special dinner together.

Jesus went to a quiet garden and prayed to God about all that was about to happen to Him.

Some people didn't believe
Jesus was God's Son,
so they had Him nailed to a cross.

When Jesus was on the cross,
the earth shook and rocks split.

Crossword Puzzle

ACROSS

2. Jesus's heavenly Father

3. How you talk to God

5. Another word for boys and girls

6. What people shouted as Jesus rode by

DOWN

1. What Jesus did to His disciples' feet

2. The place where Jesus prayed one night

4. The animal Jesus rode into Jerusalem

5. Jesus died on this

7. You pound this with a hammer

After Jesus died on the cross,
His friends buried Him in a tomb.

A few days later, some women went to the tomb. The stone was rolled away, and Jesus was not there.

An angel told the women,
"Jesus is not here. He is alive!"

One morning, Jesus met the disciples on the beach. He made breakfast for them.

Word Search

J	E	S	U	S	T	M	M	O	R	N	I	N	G
D	E	A	S	T	E	R	S	R	A	L	I	V	E
H	N	S	S	O	R	C	N	G	R	C	Y	O	J
D	G	B	E	A	C	H	D	W	R	I	S	E	N
T	L	A	N	G	E	L	N	J	N	E	M	O	W
L	F	O	L	L	O	W	E	R	S	G	D	C	R
R	G	B	H	Y	H	S	I	F	Q	R	H	N	T

Find the following words in the puzzle. Words may be forward or backward:

- ALIVE
- ANGEL
- BEACH
- CROSS
- EASTER
- FISH
- FOLLOWERS
- JESUS
- JOY
- MORNING
- RISEN
- WOMEN

The time came for Jesus to go back to heaven. He told His disciples to tell everyone about Him.

Jesus said He would send the Holy Spirit to be a special Helper to all of His followers.

Decode the Message

Using the key, decode the message.

__ __ __ __ __ __ __
20 1 2   1 12 21 13

__ __ __ __ __ __
 9 5 17 24 17 20

__ __ __ __ __
17 9 12 26 24

__ __ __ __ __ __.
 1 2 21 5 2 24

KEY	
1 = H	14 = W
2 = E	15 = X
3 = A	16 = K
4 = J	17 = I
5 = P	18 = D
6 = B	19 = N
7 = M	20 = T
8 = F	21 = L
9 = S	22 = V
10 = Z	23 = C
11 = Q	24 = R
12 = O	25 = G
13 = Y	26 = U

On Easter Sunday, we celebrate Jesus. When we believe in Him, we belong to His family.

We can praise Jesus every day and thank Him for His wonderful love.